GRANTBOOKS

GRANTBOOKS

A **BETTING GUIDE** FOR THE **2021 NFL SEASON**

EARL GRANT

GRANTBOOKS
A BETTING GUIDE FOR THE 2021 NFL SEASON

iUniverse books may be ordered through booksellers or by contacting:

iUniverse
1663 Liberty Drive
Bloomington, IN 47403
www.iuniverse.com
844-349-9409

ISBN: 978-1-6632-2672-3 (sc)
ISBN: 978-1-6632-2671-6 (e)

Library of Congress Control Number: 2021914817

Print information available on the last page.

iUniverse rev. date: 07/21/2021

This is the first published installment of Grantbooks. I started Grantbooks back in 2017. I needed a tool that possessed my thoughts of the NFL prior to the season starting. Once the season begin an NFL handicapper can we pulled in various directions.

Grantbooks will serves as your compass to stay due north towards cashing out winning tickets. All week one-point spreads come directly from the Sportsbook.

All points spread weeks 2-18 are my personal point spread projections.

- Keep in mind I assume all key players are healthy and playing

I project point spreads so I have an idea of whom I believe should be the favorite and how many points the favorite should have to cover.

Teaser Bets

Teaser Bets allow you to play a different game the Sportsbooks and other most other bettors.

Grantbooks was created to identify the cream of the crop spots for weekly teaser bets. I do not offer any positions that me and my team will not bet ourselves

Strait Bets

I am simply giving you advice on which team bet on the spread. I am not saying every single bet position is a must bet. Most betters are going to gamble with reckless irresponsibility. So, if you're going to bet every game on the board, I want to aid you in winning every bet that you place.

Moneyline Underdogs

I do not offer underdog moneyline spots that me and my team will not bet ourselves. Only betting favorites on the moneyline limits your earnings.

For Questions or Comments Contact Me at
4surefirepicks1@gmail.com
Or 719-930-6357

WEEK 1

WEEK 1

WEEK 1

Chargers @ Washington Football Team

We expect for Washington's defense to perform at a high level as they did in 2020. The defense ranked #6 in the NFL allowing 21.2 points per game. The Chargers will start multiple new faces on their offensive line. Defensive cohesiveness bonds faster than an offense. If this game was later in season and The Chargers offense had more snaps under their belt, I would be far less concerned.

Another scheduling advantage for Washington involves the visiting teams travel distance. The Chargers also make the flight from west coast time to east coast time zone. Washington will be playing their season home opening game. This element solidifies Washington's position.

William Hill Sportsbook list the line as Chargers -1. I do not find a scheduling advantage for Los Angles Week 1. The best play is to place. Washington into a teaser bet and move their point spread up. I cannot trust the Chargers to win a road game across the country in week 1. If you're going to bet the spread, back Washington.

WEEK 1
Eagles @ Falcons

This will be one of the least talked about week 1 matchups. However, thousands of betters will still find this game on their tickets. The Eagles visit the Falcons. Atlanta will be playing their season home opener. In 2020, The Falcons ranked #9 in pass play percentage. The Eagles ranked #8 in pass play percentage.

Both teams drastically favored passing the ball on offense rather than running. I do not believe either squad will stray far from their 2020 offensive philosophies. The Falcons finished dead last #32 in passing yards allowed per game. The Eagles staff will look to exploit this deficiency and air it out week 1.

The lines makers have set the over/under at 46.5. I say go over the point total. In the first game of the year, both teams will go for what they know. Airing out the football.

Yes, this is the season opener for the Falcons. However, that Is not enough help from the schedule or me to be the Falcons at -3.5. This is a road dog spot to take the Eagles for the outright win and get that plus money.

WEEK 1
Jets @ Panthers

This is the Sam Darold revenge game. In 2018, the New York Jets drafted Sam Darnold with the #3 overall pick. Darnold made 38 starts and then The Jets traded Darnold to the Panthers in April of 2021.

New York selected Zack Wilson with the #2 overall pick in the 2021 draft to replace Sam Darnold. This will be Panther's home opener. The crowd will have this stadium thick with energy. The Panthers will rally behind their QB and play with an added edge to win for Sam Darnold.

William Hill has the point spread set at -4 Panthers.

With the Sam Darnold factor, the schedule adds extra incentive for the Panthers. This is one of the better positions that you will have all year to bet the Panthers. I advise putting the Panthers in a teaser bet and moving their point spread down.

WEEK 1
Seahawks @ Colts

The Seahawks travel to play the Colts in week 1. Both franchises participated in the 2020 playoffs. The Seahawks possess major scheduling factors not in their favor. There lies significant distance traveled from Seattle to Indianapolis. The Colts will be playing their home opener of the season as well.

William Hill Sportsbooks have set the line at Colts -2.5 The plus money for taking a Seahawks strait win is not rewarding enough for the risk. And +2.5 is not enough point for me bet Seattle with the spread. I suggest betting the Colts on the money line and just pay the juice for a strait up win.

WEEK 1
49ers @ Lions

In week 1 the Lions play their home opener hosting the 49ers.

According to vegasinsider.com, the 49ers over /under season win total is set at 10.5. The Lions over/under win total sits a 5. In 2020, the 49ers won 6 games and the Lions won 5 games.

The 49ers suffered various injuries in the 2020 covid season. Starting QB Jimmy Garoppolo missed 13 games. 49ers stud defensive lineman Nick Bosa played just 2 games. The linemakers believe a healthy 49ers squad will return to the playoffs. The Lions are only projected to increase their win total by 1 game.

The Lions have a new coaching staff in place. Detroit also has a new QB understudy in Jared Goff. Goff led The Rams offense to a Super Bowl berth in 2019. Goff is still just 26 years of age.

This is not the best to road spot to try and cover two scores with the 49ers. You don't know exactly what this squad will play like in week 1. This will be the Lions home opener, and there is a chance Detroit play well.

Currently William Hill Sportsbooks list the 49ers as a -7.5 point road favorite. With all due respect to the 49ers, I find this number to be high. San Francisco trek east and a bit north to the Motor City. If you are in this game, bet the +7.5 with the Lions.

Detroit holds value in teaser adding more point to their spread.

WEEK 1
Vikings @ Bengals

The one thing I know about week 1 in the NFL, is that I don't anything. Upsets are possible. I keep this detail in mind the Vikings visit the Bengals. Cincinnati will be playing their home opener. The Bengals will have the pump of warm-blooded humans back in their stadium. William Hill Sportsbook list the Vikings as a -3-point favorite.

n 2020, the Vikings lacked the defensive integrity to keep teams out of endzone. Minnesota ranked #29 allowing 29.7 points per game. The Vikings signed a handful of free agents to upgrade their defense. I still do not trust the defense on the road week 1. The Bengals defense also played poor in 2020. Cincinnati finished #21 in points allowed, surrendering 26.5 points per game.

The Vikings at -3 may seems like an easy cover, however I need to see the Vikings pop some pads on defense before I trust them on the road. If you bet this game, taking the Bengals on the money line is the play. You will receive plus money for the Bengals straight win. This is a very winnable game for the Bengals. Placing the Bengals in a teaser and moving their point spread up is also an option.

WEEK 1
Steelers @ Bills

In week 1, the Bills play their season opener hosting the Steelers.

The Buffalo Bills secured the 2020 AFC East crown and lost in the AFC Championship game to the Chiefs. The Pittsburgh Steelers ran away with the AFC North division.

However, The Steelers playoff run never made it out of the starting block. The Browns upset the Steelers in the first round of the playoffs.

Currently William Hill Sportsbook have a line of Bills -7.5. I cannot just book the Bills to win this game by a touchdown and an additional score. You might not see the Steelers as a -7.5 point underdog again.

I am advocating that you add points to the Steelers point spread in a teaser. You should also consider betting the Steelers for a straight win on the money line you will get a return of plus money with this bet. Pittsburgh needs to be a placed in your week 1 teaser bet.

WEEK 1

Steelers @ Bills

Invest 1 unit on play that season finance on tapping the Steelers.

The Buffalo Bills lost on the 20-0 AFC East power and lost in the AFC Championship route to the Chiefs. The Pittsburgh Steelers ran away with the AFC North division.

However, The Steelers play on run never miss cut out of season time clock. The Browns beat the Steelers in the last round of the playoffs.

Currently with small Bill "prefolrok have a line -4 Bills -7.0 I cannot just in that the Bills win this game by a touchdown and an additional score. You think it's not fair the Steelers as a 7.5 point underdog again.

I am advocating that you take a point on the Steelers point spread in a teaser. You would also consider betting the Steelers for a straight win on the moneyline. The wager will give a return, thus money with that bet. The teaser bet to be placed in your week 1 teaser bet.

WEEK 2

WEEK 2

WEEK 2
Vikings @ Cardinals

In week 2, The Arizona Cardinals play host to the Minnesota Vikings. Both teams possess multiple playmakers on offense. Each club also believes they have talent to play in the post season Arizona will be playing its season home opener.

Minnesota plays in Cincinnati Week 1 verses the Bengals. The Vikings defense will be challenged by the Bengals offensive capabilities.

In week 2 the Vikings, play back-to-back road games as they fly to Arizona to take on the Cardinals. The Climate change most notably the difference in humidity is a factor working against the Vikings.

The Cardinals will be a small home favorite. I anticipate a point spread of Cardinals -2.5. Any spread -3 or less for Arizona had good value in a teaser bet. I suggest betting Arizona to strait win on the money line. The Vikings will be on back-to-back road games, and the Cardinals will be playing their home opener.

WEEK 2
Titans @ Seahawks

This game will make some waves in the media. Both the Titians and Seahawks have intentions on returning the playoffs. Each squad qualified for the 2020 playoffs and made early exits in the opening round.

Seattle plays on the road at Indianapolis Colts in week 1. I believe the Seahawks can build from playing the Colts (2020 playoff team) on the road. The adversity should make them a more resilient team in week 2.

The Seahawks possess one of the most interactive home crowds in the NFL. This will be Seattle's 2021 home opener and their fans will be lit. The raucous crowd in Seattle have been cooped up due to covid.

The Tennessee Titians plays at home week 1, hosting the Cardinals. Arizona offensively will expose holes in Titan's defense. Seattle will pick of the weaknesses the Cardinals highlight.

The Titians also must endure the travel mileage going south to the great northwest. This travel included time zone and climate changes.

The Seahawks will be slight favorites on the point spread. I do not advise you betting against that home crowd in Seattle. This game will be close you bet the Seahawks on the money line to strait up win. The Seahawks should find their way into your week 2 teaser also.

WEEK 3

WEEK 3

WEEK 3

Washington Football Team @ Bills

The Washington Football team visits the Buffalo Bills in week 3. Washington won the 2020 NFC East division. The Bills finished first place in their division as champions of the AFC East.

Coming into Week 3, The Washington Football Team will not have compiled many travel miles.

Week 1 Host Chargers
Week 2 Host Giants (NFC East division game)

The flight to Buffalo from Washington is brief. Washington plays their first two games at home. The schedule shows Washington some love as they go on the road to play the 2020 AFC runner-up Buffalo Bills.

Now let's see the Bills schedule.
Week 1 Host Steelers (2020 playoff qualifier)
Week 2 @ Dolphins (2020 playoff qualifier) (AFC East division game)

In 2020, The Steelers surrendered just 21.2 points per game. The Dolphins defense played just as brilliant, only giving up 21.1 points per game.

The Bills will see an elite defensive group for the third consecutive week. The schedule is applying premium opposition to the Bills.

The Bills will be the home favorite. If the Spread climbs over −7.5 for the Bills, the schedule makes it difficult to not back Washington. The Washington's money line should be in your underdog round robin or your underdog parlay. Adding more points with Washington is clever move I suggest placing Washington in your teaser bet as well.

WEEK 3
Falcons @ Giants

This will be The Giants second straight home game. The Giants return a defensive unit from 2020 that ranked #9 in the NFL in points. The Falcons defense finished # 19 in points allowed per game and gave up 30 points per game the last 3 games of the season.

In the early weeks of football season defense continuity gels faster than offense. The Falcons defense is not sound enough to go on the road in week 3. When I add the fact that this is the Giants second consecutive home game, this appears to be a bad spot for the Falcons. Atlanta will still be searching for ways to replace All-Pro WR Julio Jones production.

The Giants will be the favorite. I anticipate the line to be set a Giants -3. My advice is to take the Giants to win on the money line. As a home team with manageable point spread, the Giants will stand firm in a teaser bet.

WEEK 3
Saints @ Patriots

The Saints visit the Patriots for each team's third game of the season. New Orleans earned a 2020 playoff spot. New England season ended with the Patriots watching the playoffs on TV. This will be back-to-back road games for New Orleans.

The Saints play at the Carolina Panthers in week 2. New Orleans travel log gets more miles in this week 3 match up.

New England plays AFC East divisional games weeks 1 and 2.

Week 1 Host Dolphins (2020 playoff team) (AFC East division game)
Week 2 @ Jets (AFC East division game)

The accumulative effect of New England playing two division games to offset the travel of the Saints. Teams use extra time and preparation in gamelans for division games. Division games often expel high volumes of energy in a win or a loss.

New England will be the favorite. The line may be Patriots -3.5. The Schedule neutralizes enough factors to provide value for betting the Saints points as an underdog. Adding more points to Saints spread in a teaser is must. For all gamblers looking to bank plus money, the Saints money line is a strong spot bet. The Saints moneyline should be in your underdog parlay or round robin.

WEEK 3
Buccaneers @ Rams

In week 3, the Buccaneers visit the Rams in Los Angles. With the addition of former Lions QB Matt Stafford, the Rams may be best equipped to challenge the defending Super Bowl Buccaneers in the NFC.

This is the Rams schedule for the first three weeks of the season.

Week 1 host Bears (2020 playoff team)
Week 2 @ Colts (2020 playoff team)
Week 3 Host Buccaneers (2020 Super Bowl champions)

The Rams open their 2021 season, week 1 hosting the Chicago Bears (2020 Playoff Team). In week 2, the Rams fly from L.A. to Indianapolis to play the Colts (2020 Playoff Team). The Rams are gifted a lump for cool in week 3, as they host the 2020 Super Champion Tampa Bay Buccaneers.

Here is a look at the Buccaneers schedule.

Week 1 Host Cowboys
Week 2 Host Falcons

Prior to week 3, Tampa Bay plays their first two games of the season in confines of their own stadium. In terms of completion Tampa Bay's opponents are not overtly difficult. This a good spot for the Buccaneers to play road game verses a team of the Rams caliber.

The Rams should be the favorite in this game. However, I would not be surprised to see line set at Buccaneers -1.5 The Rams are 2020 playoff and have Super Bowl aspirations this season. I need to relay to you that in this spot, the Buccaneers receive loftier scheduling arrangements. I advise you to place the Buccaneers into a teaser. This fortifies the position of Tampa Bay playing the first two games of the regular season at home.

WEEK 3

Host Packers @ 49ers (Sunday Night Football)

The 49ers will play their 2021 home opener hosting the Packers. The building will we overflowing with enthusiasm form the 49ers faithful. With two games under their belt the 49ers offense will be clicking. The defense will play with fire as well. San Francisco plays on the road in their first two games of the season.

Week 1 @ Lions
Week 2 @ Eagles

The two road games to cause concern by changing times zones and the traveling miles accumulated. A well-coached team such as the 49ers, can channel adversity into building character.

In 2020, The Packers season ended with a loss in the 2020 NFC Championship. Green Bay's first two games of 2021 intel their own set of obstacles.
Week 1, Green Bay plays the Saints (2020 playoff team) in New Orleans. The Packers will have endured a hostile crowd after a lengthy flight to New Orleans.

Week 2, the Packers host the Lions for an NFC North showdown. This Is not easy a game for Green Bay. The Lions will always take their best swipe at the Packers.

The 49ers will be set as the favorite. I line could be 49ers -5. This is a Sunday Night Football game, and the 49ers home opener. San Francisco will receive a formidable boost from their fans. I Moving the 49ers spread down in teaser is the play here.

WEEK 3
Seahawks@ Vikings

In week 3, The Seahawks make a trip east to an attempt to pillage the Vikings. Last season, the Seahawks stole 27-26 victory from the Vikings. We will begin breaking down the Vikings schedule.

Week 1@Bengals
Week 2 @ Cardinals.

Week 1 The Vikings play the Bengals in Cincinnati. The Bengals offense will attack a Minnesota defense in search for their identity. The Vikings play at the Cardinals week 2. I am concerned about the Vikings recovering from the heat and humidity in Arizona.

After all, The Vikings will be playing consecutive road games against the Cardinals. The Cardinals pack a potent offense and defense returns a competitive unit that made upgrades.

Week 3 will be Minnesota's home opening game. The Seahawks will have faced the Colts on the road in Indy's home opener in week 1. I find the Minnesota's home opener advantage to lose a little steam as the Seahawks dealt with this factor in week 1. The Vikings on paper are not as strong as the Seahawks first two opponents. Now we will look at the Seahawks schedule for weeks 1 and 2.

Week 1 @ Colts (2020 playoff team)
Week 2 Host Titians (2020 playoff team)

Both the Colts and the Titans played in the 2020 playoffs. The Seahawks will be battle tested once the reach Minnesota. Seattle also plays at home week 2. The Vikings are on the road weeks 1 and 2.

Seattle may be penciled in as the favorite. If the Vikings are set as the favorite, it won't be more than -1.5 or -2.

Whatever the line is the schedule says bet Seattle. The Seahawks will be battle tested and already have experienced playing on the road going against the energy of a home opening crowd. I advise plugging the Seahawks into teaser bet.

WEEK 3

Bears @ Browns

The Browns and Bears each played in the 2020 playoffs. Cleveland plays host to Chicago in week 3. We will view the Browns schedule.

Week 1 @Cheifs (2020 AFC Champions)
Week 2 (Host Texans)

We see the Browns with the very difficult week one road game. Cleveland goes to Kansas City to battle that AFC champion chiefs. The Browns loss to the Chiefs in the divisional round of last year's playoffs. Cleveland will have an opportunity to measure themselves against the standard of the AFC when they play Kansas City.

In Week 2 Cleveland hosts Houston. The Browns will use the game against the Texans as a medium clean up mistakes from week one and to continue building towards another playoff run. I do love Cleveland playing a second consecutive home game hosting the Bears, the Browns fans will be in full force providing an extra element to combat the Bears.

The Bears will be playing their second road game in three weeks. These aren't just to average teams that they will be playing on the road.

Week 2 @ Rams (2020 playoff team)
Week 3 @ Browns (2020 playoff team)

Vegasinsider.com has the Browns and Rams season win Totals at 9.5 and 9 respectively. Currently the Bears starting QB is in question and the Browns know media darling Baker Mayfield is their guy.

You want to back the Browns if spread is no greater than -5. Cleveland had become a team that the public loves. Therefore, the opening line may be inflated. In the event the spread is higher than Browns -5. You install the Browns in a teaser moving their point spread down.

WEEK 3
Ravens @ Lions

We have two teams with opposites trajectories in this matchup. The Baltimore Ravens have built a championship contending unit. The Detroit Lions are building a team that can simply just be competitive. The Lions host the Ravens in week 3 of the regular season.

The Ravens play at the Raiders in Las Vegas during week 1. This game will require an extensive flight from Baltimore to Las Vegas. In Week 2, the Ravens host the 2020 AFC champion Kansas City Chiefs. The Ravens trip to Detroit in week 3, will serve as one of the least traveled road games of the season for Baltimore. I believe this scheduling position is Favorable for the Ravens.

In week 1, the Lions play their season opener hosting the San Francisco 49ers. In Week 2, Detroit makes a short trip to Green Bay to duel with the Packers. The Lions at Packers is an NFC North Division game. I cannot locate with any element of the Lions schedule that enhances their position.

The sportsbooks will set the Ravens as giant road favorites. I am expecting to see a point spread of Ravens- 10. I don't love a high spread like this for road teams. At -10 you just bet the Ravens in first half wager.

If the line is set a -7, I will say got bet on the Ravens. You do have a solid position placing the Ravens in a teaser and moving there spread down.

WEEK 3
Jets @ Broncos

In week 3, The Broncos host the New York Jets. It will be interesting to see the quality of play that these teams will put on the field. The Jets flight to Denver is extensive. New York will also have to contented when the thin air and extreme altitude in Denver. The Jets went 2-14 in 2020, this trip to Denver is set up as a formidable challenge.

The Broncos will be playing in their season home opener. Denver's 2020 home record stood at a distasteful 2-6. Defending home field will be a point of emphasis in 2021. The Broncos crowd will be and provide an off the field factor. The high attitude and thin air in Denver, adds another condition for the Jets to contend with. This is likely the strongest home game spot to bet the Broncos in 2021.

Expect the Broncos to be -4.5-point favorites. I have nothing personal against the Jets. However, there is no way I am backing the Jets. Bet the Broncos on the point spread. Denver is also a good candidate to be placed in your teaser.

WEEK 4

WEEK 4

WEEK 4
Chiefs @ Eagles

The Eagles make a trip to Kansas City for a week 4 contest with the Chiefs.

The Eagles play at The Dallas Cowboys in week 3. The Eagles will leave their heads and hearts in Dallas with either a win or loss. As NFC East rivals, Philly and Dallas push themselves to brink. The Chiefs will be pumped up for Andy Reid's return to the Philadelphia. Reid served as the Head Coach for the Eagles from 2005-2012.

I would normally question if Kansas City would have the vested interest in to cover as heavy road favorite in this spot. However, the schedule provides KC with the proper motivation in week 4.

The Andy Reid factor is a quirk in the schedule that you do not get every year. Kansas City will be slated as the favorite. Bet the Chiefs on the point spread. Kansas City may have point spread at -7. Take the Chiefs spread down, and you will have a lock in your teaser.

WEEK 4

Buccaneers @ Patriots (Sunday Night Football)

Buccaneers at Patriots is billed as the Sunday Football game. The Patriots also lose the bulletin board material edge for this contest.

The Buccaneers Tom Brady is returning to New England for the first time to play his former employer.

Brady led New England to five Super Wins. Brady joined the Buccaneers in last season after an ugly divorce with the New England. Tom Brady served has the conduit that surged Tampa Bay to the 2020 Playoffs. The Buccaneers won all four of their playoff games in route becoming 2020 Super Bowl Champions.

The Patriots will be playing a third 2020 playoff team in four weeks. We need to check out the Patriots Schedule

Week 1 Host Dolphins (2020 playoff team) (AFC East division game)
Week 2 @ Jets (AFC East division game)
Week 3 Host Saints (2020 playoff team)
Week 4 Host Buccaneers (2020 Super Bowl champions)

I am concerned that New England's first three opponents do not feature a topflight QB. The schedule is working against the Patriots in this regard. The defense will be testing by an elite QB. Even a good defense can be shell shocked when they finally encounter an elite Quarterback.

This seems like a good spot to bet the Buccaneers on the road. I am expecting a point spread of Tampa Bay -5. As long is the spread being Buccaneers -5 or less, I am in with Tampa Bay. I advise incorporating New England into a teaser bet.

WEEK 4
Browns @ Vikings

The Browns are franchise with plans to build of their 2020 playoff appearance and make a deep run into the playoffs. The Vikings will need to improve the play of their defense to reach the playoffs in 2021.

The Vikings will be playing back-to-back home games in week 4.
Week 3 Host Seahawks (2020 playoff team)
Week 4 Host Browns (2020 playoff team)

I find the Vikings week 3 game versus the Seahawks to be a perfect to tune-up game to host the Browns. Seattle's offense can score in bunches and create big plays. Also, Minnesota is difficult place for out of conference teams like the Browns to earn a win.

The Browns play two home games in weeks 2-3, then flying to Minnesota. The Browns possess question marks in their secondary and will breaking in new faces. In 2020, Cleveland ranked #22 in points allowed per game. The Browns gave up 26.6 points per game. Minnesota may be able to score early and often.

Cleveland may be slight road favorites in this matchup. This point spread will be dependent upon the Vikings first three contests. We could see a line set as Browns -2.5 or the Vikings could retain the home field advantage and be favored at -2.5. Either way the public betters will view this game as an easy grab for the Browns. The Vikings are the play here. The back-to-back home games for Vikings will be proved to be worth their weight in gold.

WEEK 4
Steelers @ Packers

In week 4, a clash of kings will be brewing in the Green Bay. The AFC North Champion Steelers visit the NFC North Champion Packers. The schedule will provide insight on which team to lean on.

We will start with Steeler's collection of opponents for weeks 1-3.

Week 1 @ Bills (2020 AFC runner up)
Week 2 Host Raiders
Week 3 Host Bengals (AFC north division game)

Pittsburgh's week 1 road game at Buffalo (2020 AFC runner up) stands out as their stiffest challenge. The Bengals finished last in the AFC North; the Steelers play the weakest of their divisional opponents. The Steelers also play consecutive home games prior to the road game in Green Bay. There are not any additional scheduling elements offering the Steelers resistance.

Green Bay plays two road games in their first three weeks of the season. The week 3 game in San Francisco is troubling. Troubling in the terms of the Packers shifting from the central time zone and hiking out west to San Francisco. The Steelers stay home in Pittsburgh, while Packer's head out west.

The Packers should be -3.5 favorites in this contest. I do not find a scheduling advantage to push me to bet either squad on the point spread. I will suggest entering the Steelers in a teaser bet, this move puts you in solid stance with the Steelers.

WEEK 4
Texans @ Bills

The Bills host the Texans in week 4. This spot is less about the Texans schedule and more about the Bills. Let's have a look at Buffalos schedule. The Bills will be playing their third home game within a four-week window.

Week 1 Host Steelers (2020) playoff team)
Week 2 @ Dolphins (2020 playoff team) (AFC East division game)
Week 3 Host Washington (2020 playoff team)

Unfortunately, Buffalo starts their season playing three consecutive 2020 playoff teams. Week 1, the Bills contend with the reigning AFC North Champion Pittsburgh Steelers. Week 2 features an AFC East Division contest with the Miami Dolphins.

Week 3, the Washington Football Team invades Buffalo in search of a road upset. Washington won the NFC East division in 2020. The Bills benefit from playing the Texans during his home stand in Buffalo. The Bills could struggle to enter week 4 with a losing a record. The Texans may be on the wrong side of a must win game for the Bills.

The Bills should be set as the favorites. The Point spread should be set at Bills -10.5. This a large point spread. However, a battle tested Bills squad can run away with this game. I won't bet a spread over Bills -9.5. I want 10 points to be a cover for the Bills. I will however place the Bills in a teaser and move their point spread down. The Bills first half is wager worth looking into.

WEEK 4

Colts @ Dolphins

Welcome to Miami! The Dolphins Host the Colts in week 4. These two franchises each made the 2020 playoffs. Indianapolis first four games appear more trying than any other team in the league. Here's a look.

Week 1 Host Seahawks (2020 playoff team)
Week 2 Host Rams (2020 playoff team)
Week 3 @ Titians (2020 playoff team) (AFC south division game)
Week 4 @ Dolphins (2020 Playoff Team)

Once the Colts meet the Dolphins, Indianapolis will be playing their fourth consecutive 2020 playoff team. Each team weeks 1-3 offer a different challenge and all three of these teams will likely be back in the playoffs. I really don't believe the Colts will be at their best once they play the Dolphins.

Miami will be home favorites. A fair line will be Dolphins -3. I won't like anything higher than Dolphins -4. This is a juicy spot for the Dolphins. The schedule says bet the Dolphins on the point spread. Your teaser should include the Dolphins, teasing their point spread down. The Dolphins first half is a wager to consider also.

WEEK 5

WEEK 5

Saints @ Washington Football Team

Two 2020 playoff teams collide as the Washington Football team host the New Orleans Saints. Currently neither franchise has designated whom will be their starting quarterbacks. New Orleans will be playing their third road game in four weeks.

Week 2 @ Panthers (NFC South division game)
Week 3@ Patriots
Week 4 Host Giants

I prefer to have strong QB play and a strong to defense to play this type of road schedule. The Saints do not have the quality QB play for me to trust them in week 5 at the Washington. The trip to Washington will be a third east coast flight in four weeks for the Saints. It's far too early into the season to trust the Saints offense be efficient under these circumstances.

This is Washington's week 3-4 schedule
Week 3 @ Bills (2020 AFC runner up)
Week 4 @ Falcons

Washington will travel week 3 playing away vs the Bills. Buffalo lost in last year's AFC Champions game to Kansas City. The Falcons won 4 games in 2020, sportsbooks could set Washington as the favorite in Atlanta. The Falcons appear to be trending down for 2021, Washington will build of the Falcons game.

I do not foresee a line higher than -3 for Washington as a home favorite. I cannot bet the Saints and fall victim to losing the turnover battle. Washington will hold strong in a teaser bet moving their point spread down.

WEEK 5
Eagles @Panthers

The Eagles visit Carolina to scrap with the Panthers. This game will not receive much hype for the media. The schedule will still point you in the direction of a sweet bet.

Looking at the Panthers schedule we see that Carolina plays on the road in weeks 3 and 4.

Week 3 @ Texans
Week 4 @ Cowboys

The Eagles play at home week 4 and their travel milage from Philadelphia to Carolina is very light. I don't love the Panthers traveling south in weeks 3 and 4. I find the Eagles and Panthers to be evenly matched on paper. The traveling schedule to benefits the visiting Eagles in this spot.

I expect the Panthers to a light home favorite. Maybe the line gets set at Panthers -2 or -3. With the aid of the schedule, single betting Philadelphia on the moneyline or plus money carries more reward than risk. Adding more points to Eagles with a teaser is a wise move.

WEEK 5
Dolphins @ Buccaneers

Tampa Bay host Miami in a week 5 contest. The Dolphins finished the 2020 season strong and locked down a bid to the playoffs. The Buccaneers ended their season winning the Super Bowl.

Let's have a gander at the Dolphins schedule

Week 1 @ Patriots (AFC East division game)
Week 2 Host Bills (AFC runner up) (division game)
Week 3 @ Raiders (West Coast Road trip)
Week 4 Host Colts (2020 playoff team)
Week 5 @ Buccaneers (2020 Super Bowl champions)

The Miami Dolphins are shown no mercy thorough the first five weeks of their schedule. Miami will play three playoff teams in five weeks. Miami also will compete in two AFC East division games.

Miami played the Raiders in week 16 last season. The loser of the game would be eliminated from playoff contention. The Dolphins flipped by winning 26-25. Miami plays the Raiders in Las Vegas in week 3. You got to believe the Raiders will be enter the matchup with extra steam in their engines. I see far too many elements of the schedule adding resistance to this spot for the Dolphins.

As I poke holes in the schedule for the Tampa Bay. Prior to this game versus Miami. The Buccaneers do play two consecutive road games.

Week 3 @ Rams (2020 playoff team)
Week 4 @ Patriots

In their first 5 games, Tampa Bay plays just 1 division game and 1 (2020) playoff team. The Buccaneers have stout road test in week 3 with the Rams. In 2020, the Rams ranked # 2 in scoring defense. Miami ranked #4 in scoring defense. Tampa will have already seen an elite defense vs the Rams.

This will be one of the better spots to bet the Buccaneers at home. Due to inflation the Buccaneers spreads will get higher. I foresee a line of Tampa Bay -5.5. With the Buccaneers on the spread -6 is high as I am willing to go. Due to the Dolphins brutal schedule weeks 1-4, this also a prime opportunity to bet the Buccaneers in the first half as well.

WEEK 5

Colts @ Ravens (Monday Night Football)

The Indianapolis Colts visit the Baltimore Ravens. This matchup will be featured on Monday Night Football. Each franchise qualified for the 2020 playoff field. The is an early season to see where each team stands

Prior to week 5, Baltimore plays two consecutive games on the road.

Week 3 @ Lions
Week 4 @ Broncos

Baltimore's week 3 trip to Detroit is lenient as far as miles traveled. The Ravens road trip to Denver consist of the change from eastern to mountain standard time zone. The Broncos can hand the Ravens loss. Returning home to host the Colts, allows the Ravens exuberant crowd to provide a lift.

Indianapolis will be playing their third consecutive road contest. The Ravens will also serve as the fifth consecutive 2020 playoff opponent for the Colts.

Week 1 Host Seahawks (2020 playoff team)
Week 2 Host Rams (2020 playoff team)
Week 3 @Titain (2020 playoff team) (AFC South division game)
Week 4 @ Dolphins (2020 playoff team)
Week 5 @ Ravens (2020 playoff team)

The residual effect of such a brutal schedule becomes the Colts worse enemy in week 5. Indianapolis plays the most demanding first five games in the entire NFL. Not The Colt receive absolutely no help from the schedule.

This not the week to bet with Indianapolis. Baltimore will the favorites. The line could open as high as Ravens -6. I suggest betting the Ravens on point spread. This is also a position to wager on the Ravens first half. Baltimore should absolutely be in your teaser bet, moving the Ravens point spreads down. The Ravens first half wager is mandatory.

WEEK 6

WEEK 6

WEEK 6
Rams @ Giants

The Los Angeles Rams visit the New York Giants in week 6. New York aims to re-group after posting a 6 -10 record a year ago. The Rams are confident that they can make a run at the Super Bowl.

In Weeks 2-5 the Rams play one of the more treacherous leagues wide schedules. Let's have a look.

Week 2 @ Colts (2020 playoff team)
Week 3 Host Buccaneers (2020 Super Bowl champions)
Week 4 Host Cardinals (NFC West division game)
Week 5 @ Seahawks (2020 playoff Team) (NFC West division game)

This is challenging run. I question the emotional balance of the Rams after back-to-back division games with the Cardinals and the Seahawks. Next, they fly from L.A. o the east coast time zone in New York. I see this as a trap game for the Rams.

This is damn good spot for the Giants as a home underdog. Oddsmakers will place the Rams as the favorite. I am projecting a line of Rams -5. I find this to be prime spot to take the points you will get with New York. For those who love risk versus reward bets. The money line bet with Giants is the play. This will be a game in which the majority of analyst will give the Giants zero chance to win.

WEEK 6
Cardinals @ Browns

The Cleveland Browns host the Cardinals in week 6. Both teams play stressful schedules entering week 6. This game features a battle of former #1 overall picks in Cardinals QB Kyler Murray and Browns QB Baker Mayfield.

This contest will be Arizona's third road game in four weeks
Week 3 @ Jaguars
Week 4 @ Rams (2020 playoff team)
Week 5 Host 49ers
Week 6 @Browns

Arizona's week 3 trip to Jacksonville racks up travel miles, and a change from Mountain Standard to Eastern Standard time zone.

In week, 4 Arizona plays in Los Angles for an NFC West division game with the Rams.

Week 5, the Cardinals play another NFC west games at home against the 49ers the two division back-to-back Division games will tax Arizona.

The Browns play two consecutive road games prior to week 6.

Week 4 @ Vikings
Week 5 @ Cardinals

The Browns play on the road in Minnesota in week 4. In week 5, the Browns make take a quite lengthy flight to Los Angles to play the Chargers. The Browns will have to adjust from a Central Standard time zone to Pacific Standard time zone. The Browns will gain fatigue from the heat and humidity in Las Angles as well. The residual impact will carry over to the following week hindering the Browns.

The schedule provides enough assistance for the Cardinals to win a close game. Cleveland will be the favorite. The spread should be Browns -5. Betting on Arizona with the point spread is the play. The Cardinals will also hold strong in a teaser bet.

WEEK 6

Seahawks @Steelers (Sunday Night Football)

The Steelers host the Seahawks in the Sunday Night Football game. The Steelers won the AFC North division and collected an automatic berth into the 2020 playoffs. The Seahawks punched their ticket to 2020 playoffs by winning NFC West division title.

The Steelers will be playing their fourth home game in five weeks! A look at this homestand for Pittsburgh will help my analysis.

Week 2 Host Raiders
Week 3Host Bengals (AFC North division game)
Week 4 @ Packers (2020 playoff team)
Week 5 Host Broncos

During this stretch, Pittsburgh plays just one AFC South division game and one 2020 playoff team. The Steelers only leave out of state Pennsylvania once as well. The Steelers are gifted comfortable circumstances from the schedule.

Seattle will be playing their third road game in four weeks.

Week 3 @ Vikings
Week 4 @ 49ers (NFC West division game)
Week 5 Host Rams (2020 playoff team) (NFC West division game)

The week 3 flight to Minnesota and the two consecutive NFC West games are hurdles that will tax the Seahawks prior to competing against the Steelers. The Rams bounced the Seahawks out of the 2020 playoffs grounding the Seahawks with a 30-20 beating. The Seahawks may leave to much their collective soul on the field in Seattle with the Rams game. They follow the Rams game with a lengthy flight to Pittsburgh.

The schedule provides the edge to the Steelers. I anticipate a point spread of Steelers – 2.5 or –3. I suggest you bet on the Steelers. After Seattle's week 5 game with the Rams, the Seahawks will not be 100 percent emotionally invested into this game. Once again this will the Seahawks third road game in four weeks.

WEEK 6

Bengals @ Lions

The Lions host the Bengals during week 6, this game features teams that both finished last in their respective divisions. Each Franchise will employ different methods to establish a culture of winning.

Cincinnati's plays at home in weeks 4 and 5.

Week 4 Host Jaguars
Week 5 Host Packers (2020 playoff game)

The Bengals and Jaguars is a game in which both teams present equal talent. At worst the Bengals will be able to gain some confidence from this contest.

The Bengals will not be weary of miles traveled due to road games; this is plus for week 6. Cincinnati's fight to Detroit is short and sweet. The Bengals receive a tangible boost from the schedule.

Unfortunately, the Lions schedule is not as forgiving as the Bengals schedule.

Week 3 Host Ravens (2020 playoff team)
Week 4 @ Bears (2020 playoff team) (NFC North division game)
Week 5 @ Vikings (NFC North division game)

Detroit must endure a physical game with Ravens in week 3. I am very alarmed that the Lions play division game on the road in weeks 4 and 5. The Lions will be underdogs in each contest. I must reiterate how much voltage is needed to compete in division games on the road. I do not foresee the Lions boasting a thunderous roar in week 6. This is a young inexperienced team; they won't be able to reset their emotions for the Bengals.

The Lions should be favorites at -1 or -2. I advise betting on the Bengals to win outright on the money line. In a teaser bet, I suggest moving the Bengals point spread. This is a quality spot bet for Cincinnati.

WEEK 6

Bills @ Titians (Monday Night Football)

The week 6 Monday Night Football game features a clash of 2020 AFC division champions. The AFC East champions Bills, travel to play the AFC South champion Titians.

We will start with the Bills schedule.

Week 3 Host Washington football team (2020 playoff Team)
Week 4 Host Texans
Week 5 @ Chiefs (2020 AFC champions)
Week 6 @ Titians (2020 playoff team)

The Chiefs game in Kansas City, followed by the Titans game in Tennessee raises red flags. Buffalo may win against the Chiefs at the expense of dropping the game versus the Titans. Kansas City is one of the most problematic venues for a visiting team to play. I am not confident that the Bills defense can hold serve against the Titans after being stretched to the seam by the Chiefs.

Now let's put some eyes on the Titians schedule

Week 4 @ Jets
Week 5 @ Jaguars (AFC South Division Game)

Tennessee plays consecutive road games in weeks 4 and 5. The schedule is more than kind to Titans. The sum of milage that Tennessee travels to New York and Jacksonville could be worse. In 2020, The Jaguars compiled a 1-15 record. The Jets finished 2020 with a 2-15 record. The Titians enter week 6 in a more than favorable position.

The Titans should be set as the favorites. Titans -1.5, or -2 will likely be the spread. If you want advice on the point spread, take the Titans. Tennessee holds stronger in a teaser bet opposed to Buffalo. The Bills are coming of a game in Kansas City that is a Sunday Night Football Game. Buffalo may look good versus the Chiefs. Do not overreact and ignore the scheduling advantage for the Titians.

WEEK 6

Chargers @ Ravens

The Baltimore Ravens will be hosting their second consecutive road game as they host the Los Angeles Chargers. The Baltimore Ravens focused on returning to the playoffs after a successful 2020 season. The Chargers have a new head coach is still l in the process of establishing a culture of waiting.

Los Angeles possess a menacing schedule week 1 through 5 there may have them softened once they reached Baltimore in week 6.

Week 1 @ Washington (2020 playoff team)
Week 2 Host Cowboys
Week 3 @ Chiefs (2020 AFC champion) (AFC West division game)
Week 4 Host Raiders (AFC West division game)
Week 5 Host Browns (2020 playoff Team)

In week 3, the Chargers play an AFC West division game in Kansas City versus Chiefs. Week 4, the Chargers play another AFC West division game at home against the Las Vegas Raiders. Weeks 3 and 4 are high stake division games for an unproven Chargers squad. In week 5, the Chargers host the Cleveland Browns. The Browns successfully won their 2020 wild card playoff game in return all their key players on this year's squad.

Once Los Angeles plays Baltimore in week 6, the Chargers will be playing their fourth 2020 playoff team in a matter of six weeks! I also must mention that the Chargers we will fly east and suffer from a climate change in Baltimore and must adjust from Pacific to East Coast Standard Time zone.

The Ravens do not play any divisional games weeks one through five. Divisional games require extra attention to detail as you play teams in your division twice per year. These games also include regional rivalries such as the LA chargers and the Las Vegas Raiders. Therefore, the emotion and energy poured into division games out way games outside of division. The Ravens play just two 2020 playoff teams in their first five games. This is a solid spot for Baltimore.

Baltimore will be set as the favorite. The point spread may be set as high as Ravens -7.5. According to the schedule, this one of The Ravens golden home spots. I advise betting the Ravens on the point spread. Baltimore's spread moved down in teaser is power play as well.

WEEK 7

WEEK 7

WEEK 7
Saints @ Seahawks

The Seattle Seahawks play host to New Orleans Saints. These two teams participated in 2020 playoffs and both squads plan on returning to the playoffs. I am curious as to whom will be the Saints starting QB. At the conclusion of the 2020 season Drew Brees retired. The Saints will be into week 7 of hoping they found his successor.

Prior to week 7, Seattle possesses a three-week window of playing very talented teams. This route includes two NFC West divisional games. Let's have look the Seahawks path to week 7.

Week 4 @ 49ers (NFC West division game)
Week 5 Host Rams (2020 NFL playoff team) (NFC West division game)
Week 6 @ Steelers

The Seahawks have their work cut out for them weeks 4 -6. Seattle plays NFC West division games in weeks 4 and 5. The 49ers and the Rams are both teams blessed with enough talent to win the NFC West. Division games require the upmost amount of focus and effort. The Seahawks will then make an extensive flight to Pittsburgh, to play the Steelers.

While the Seahawks go to Pittsburgh in Week 6, the Saints have a whole week to game plan for the Seahawks.

The Saints will have bye in week 6. This week allows New Orleans to be fresh the collective mind and body of the team.

Linemakers will position Seattle as the favorites. The point spread could be Seahawks -6. This is a spot in which you want to Bet the Saints on with the point spread. New Orleans will be the underdog. Insert New Orleans into your teaser bet and move their point spread up.

WEEK 7

Colts @49ers (Sunday Night Football)

The Indianapolis Colts fly west to play the San Francisco 49ers. This will be the Sunday Night Football game of the week. The 49ers enjoy their bye in week 6 and will have an entire week to strategize for the Colts.

Weeks 1-6 for the Colts may be the most problematic 6 week run the NFL this year. Let's put our eyes on the Colts schedule. The Colts play five 2020 playoff teams and two AFC South games.

Week 1 Host Seahawks (2020 playoff team)
Week 2 Host Rams (2020 playoff team)
Week 3 @ Titans (Division game) (2020 Playoff team)
Week 4 @ Dolphins (2020 playoff team)
Week 5 @ Ravens (2020 playoff team)
Week 6 host Texans (AFC South division game)
Week 7 @49ers

Weeks 3-6, Indianapolis plays three consecutive playoff teams on the road. I have not seen another team play 3 connective road games verses 2020 playoff teams. In week 7 at San Francisco, The Colts will be playing their fourth road game in five weeks. The schedule is no way favoring the Colts. To add insult to injury, the Colts must travel far west. And once again, the 49ers have a bye in week 6.

The 49ers should set as the favorites. The line could be set at 49ers -6. A rested 49ers team may open to fast, against Colts unit back on the road. The 49ers first half is bet is worth looking into. The 49ers are lock play in a teaser bet. The scheduling factors are too one sided in favor of the 49ers, I cannot bet the Colts.

WEEK 7
Texans @ Cardinals

In week 7, The Houston Texans matchup with The Arizona Cardinals. Five-time All-Pro Defensive Lineman JJ Watt will be playing his first season as a Cardinal. Watt spent his first ten seasons with the Texans franchise. Three-time All-Pro Wide Receiver Deandre Hopkins is in his second year with Arizona. Hopkins suited up as Texan for the first seven years of his career.

Here is a look at Texans schedule. The Texans are slated to be playing their third road game in four weeks.

Week 4 @ Bills (2020 AFC runner up)
Week 5 Host Patriots
Week 6 @ Colts (2020 Playoff team) (AFC South division game)
Week 7 @ Cardinals

The Texans fly northeast in weeks 4 and 6. The distance traveling to a different region is a concern. The Bills and the Colts participated in last year's playoffs. This window of games shows the Texans no love at all.

The Cardinals are on a favorable perch hosting the Texans. Arizona plays at home in week 5, and on the road in Cleveland in 6. This game with the Texans marks the Arizona playing their second home game in three weeks.

Week 5 Host 49ers (NFC West division game)
Week 6 @ Browns (2020 playoff team)
Week 7 Host Texans

In week 7, the schedule hammers the Texans with another quality opponent on the road. The Cardinals are in favorable position. I always attempt to project the point spread. I will use Cardinals -5.5 as my projected line. Do not be afraid to bet Arizona as high as -7.5

The Cardinals should make your teaser moving their spread down.

WEEK 7
Chiefs @ Titians

One of the marquee matchups of the week seven schedule features the Kansas City Chiefs visiting the Tennessee Titans. The Chiefs and the Titans look increase their success in 2020. This game will grab national headlines, so let's get our research started now. We will start off breaking down the Chiefs schedule.

Week 5 Host Bills (2020 AFC runner up)
Week 6 @ Washington (2020 playoff team)-
Week 7 @ Titians 2020 playoff team)

This piece of Kansas City's schedule comes with a great deal of attrition. Once Kansas City plays Tennessee, the Chiefs will be playing their third consecutive 2020 playoff team. This spot also marks back-to-back road games for the Chiefs as well. In week 5, Kansas City host the Buffalo Bills. This will be a rematch of the 2020 AFC championship game. This spot in week 7 does not hold favorable circumstances for the Kansas City Chiefs.

The Titans will be playing their second consecutive game at home. No team in the NFL wants to play the Chiefs in Kansas City. The Titans are gifted home field advantage to take a crack at the defending AFC champions.

This point spread will be interesting to track. Do not be surprised if the Chiefs are set as the favorite. I can see line being set as Chiefs -3 I do like Tennessee at home as an underdog, I advise betting them on the money line for plus money. The Titians need to be a teaser bet also.

WEEK 8

WEEK 8
Eagles @ Lions

In week 8, the Lions host the Eagles. A year ago, Detroit and Philadelphia each placed last in their respective divisions. This will be the Eagles third road contest in four weeks.

Week 5 @ Panthers
Week 6 Host Buccaneers
Week 7 @ Raiders
Week 8 @ Lions

I am very concerned with Eagles traveling west to Las Vegas in week 8 and then to Detroit in week 9. I believe the Lions get enough from the schedule to get an outright win. This is also a stellar spot to put the Lions into a teaser as well. If for some reason the Lions are a home underdog, I absolutely love the plus money for the Lions.

Week 7 Host Washington Football Team (2020 playoff team)

The scheduling gods grant Dallas some help in this contest. I find this to be a strong spot to bet the Cowboys. I get to this spread early before the Cowboys betting audience drive the lineup. This is a strong spot to place Dallas in your teaser also. I believe this spread should be Dallas -5. I am willing to bet Dallas even at -6.5

WEEK 8

Jaguars @ Seahawks

In Week 8, the Seahawks host the Jaguars. Last season, Jacksonville finished with the worst record in the NFL. In 2020, Seattle won the NFC West notching another playoff appearance. Jacksonville needs rookie QB Trevor Lawrence to display a rookie learning curve like Russell Wilsons first season. In 2012, Wilson threw for 26 Touchdown to just 10 interceptions.

The Seahawks have three primetime games scheduled prior to hosting the Jaguars.

Week 5 Host Rams (Thursday Night Football) (2020 playoff team) (NFC West division game)
Week 6 @ Steelers (Sunday Night Football) (2020 playoff team)
Week 7 Host Saints (Monday Night Football (2020 playoff team)

All three opponents during this stretch played in the 2020 playoffs. I must question how much juice the Seahawks will have in reserve to face the Jaguars. It's human nature to fall a bit flat after playing three consecutive prime time TV games. The Seahawks will be huge favorites against the Jaguars.

The milage travel from Jacksonville to Seattle reads as glaring concern. The scheduling gods must have shared this same sentiment. The Jaguars are afforded a bye in week 7! Now we look at the Jaguars schedule.

Week 5 Host Titans (2020 playoff team) (AFC South division game)
Week 6 Host Dolphins (2020 playoff team)
Week 7 Bye Week

The Jaguars will be home underdogs to the Titans and the Dolphins. The Titians and Dolphins return all their key players from 2020, as both teams reached the playoffs. Yes, Jaguars have their hands full. Playing two strong teams allow Jacksonville to be familiar with the level of competition they will see in Seattle. The Jaguars will have been at home for three weeks before leaving to play the Seahawks. The third being a week off for their bye, in week 7.

I believe the Seahawks will be favored by more than touchdown. I can see the line opening as high as -10.5 Seahawks. Seattle is clearly the stronger team. Jacksonville receives more strength from the scheduling quirks. I advise that you bet the point spread with Jaguars.

WEEK 8
Packers @ Chiefs

The Kansas City Chiefs will be playing back-to-back home games, as they host the Green Bay Packers in week 9. Green Bay intends to repeat as NFC North champ, however a Super Bowl bid the end game for the Packers.

Arrowhead stadium provides and unruly home crowd that creates noise levels that mystifies the opponent.

Scheduling conditions for Green Bay entering are quite troubling.

The Packers will be playing their third road contest within a four-week time frame. This trend warrants a look at the Packers schedule.

Week 6 @ Bears (2020 playoff Team) (NFC North division game)
Week 7 Host Washington Football Team (2020 playoff team)
Week 8 @ Cardinals
Week 9 @ Chiefs

Unfortunately, Green Bay will have defeat condition of their schedule to hold court with Kansas City. I assess the physical toll of the humidity in Arizona taxing the Packers and rolling over into week 9. These are not ideal circumstances for the Packers.

Kansas City will be set as the favorite. The line may start as high as Chiefs -5.5. The spread could be higher. I really find this to be a terrible position to bet on Green Bay. I am willing to bet the Chiefs with a line as high as -10. A first half wager for the Chiefs seems to be in order also.

WEEK 8

Patriots @ Chargers

The New England Patriots book a trip out West, to face the Los Angeles Chargers in week 8. The Patriots will endure one of their most difficult role games of the season in terms of miles traveled. This is the Patriots, moving from eastern Standard Time zone all the way to Pacific Standard Time zone as well. The Chargers, however, have their bye in week 7 and have an entire week to rejuvenate their bodies and perfect their game plan to host the Patriots.

The Chargers should be a small favorite. Chargers -2 is line I expect to see. The schedule favors Los Angeles, The Chargers. should be considered for you week 8 teaser. You want to take the home team off a bye week. The grueling flight for New England adds to the strong spot for the Chargers.

WEEK 8
Bengals @ Jets

This game will not be the topic of discussion in week 8. However, I am interested in the progression of these two franchises. The Bengals are rebuilding behind the #1 overall pick of the 2020 draft, QB Joe Burrows. The Jets selected QB Zack Wilson with the #2 overall pick in this year's draft.

The Jets have a Bye in week 6. In week 7, New York plays and an AFC East division game at The New England Patriots. These are decent circumstances for the Jets. New York's lift to Foxboro to play New England logs minute miles traveled.

The Bengals schedule is not very kind at all.

Week 6 @ Lions
Week 7 @ Ravens (2020 playoff Team) (AFC North division game)
Week 8 @ Jets

Cincinnati plays a dreaded three consecutive road games. The tail end of the road trip ending in New York versus the Jets. I really find this to be a problematic spot for the for Bengals. The week 7 match up in Baltimore, will likely have the Bengals licking their wounds before they reach New York.

The Jets should be favored at –3, or possibly –2.5. The Bengals will be at the end of three consecutive road games. In this spot, the schedule suggest that you take the Jets on the point spread. Do not overlook New York, moving their spread down in a teaser is also a winning move.

WEEK 9

WEEK 9

Falcons@ Cowboys

Week 10 The Atlanta's Road contest at Dallas will be their third road game in weeks. Let's peek at the Falcons 3 game slate prior to week 10.

Week 7 @ Dolphins (2020 playoff team)
Week 8 Host Panthers (NFC South division game)
Week 9 @ Saints (2020 playoff team) (NFC South division game)

Atlanta will only be favored in the week 8 game as they host the Panthers. The Falcons and Panthers play in the same division. Divisional games are unpredictable and highly competitive. Week 7 and 9, the Falcons on the road against 2020 playoff teams. Both the Dolphins and the Saints field strong defensive units. In 2020, New Orleans ranked 3rd in points allowed, Miami ranked 4th.

Meanwhile, The Cowboys will be at home for back-to-back home games. Since the Cowboys Bye in week 7, Dallas will have been at home three out four weeks. The schedule supplies Dallas with more leverage for the Matchup with the Falcons. You take the line the odd makers give. It could be Dallas -7. Either way I am in with Cowboys. This spot for Dallas should be in your teaser as well.

WEEK 9
Raiders @ Giants

The Las Vegas Raiders well travel to the east coast to take on the New York Giants. Normally this type of milage and time zone adjustment works again the visitor. However, the Raiders bye come one week prior in week 8.

While the Raiders are resting and game planning, the Giants make a troublesome trip to Kansas City. The defending AFC Champion Chiefs have a sizable home field advantage at Arrowhead Stadium.

The schedule eases the blow of the Raiders away game travel and give them the edge.

The Raiders should be -3 favorites. The scheduling quirks made it difficult to lay money on the Giants. I do not believe teasing the Giants up at home is sound play either.

WEEK 9

Vikings @ Ravens

The Baltimore Ravens hosts the Minnesota Vikings in week 9. The Ravens intend to make their third consecutive playoff appearance with QB Lamar Jackson leading charge. The Vikings will be striving for a road win to solidify themselves as a playoff contender.

I have done my best to build the drama of the game and the bus stops here.

The Ravens need to send gift baskets to the scheduling committee for this spot in week 9. The Ravens do not leave Baltimore during weeks 5-9! Now we need to look at this window of games on the schedule.

Week 5 Host Colts (2020 playoff team)
Week 6 Host Chargers
Week 7 Host Bengals (AFC North Division Game)
Week 8 Bye Week

Baltimore plays just one 2020 playoff team in this five-week window, and only one division game as well. Ravens head coach John Harbaugh is 9-5 against the point spread when coming off a bye week.

Perhaps this line is set at Ravens -7.5, it could be higher. With a healthy Ravens team there is nothing that will get me to take the points with Vikings. For those of you that compile teaser bets, the Ravens are a must play.

WEEK 9
Jets @ Colts

In week 9, the Jets head to the Midwest to play the Indianapolis Colts.

If the Colts are going return to the playoffs, they will need to survive a herculean first 8 weeks of their schedule.

Week 1 Host Seahawks (2020 playoff team)
Week 2 Host Rams (2020 playoff team)
Week 3 @ Titans (2020 playoff team) (AFC South division game)
Week 4 @ Dolphins (2020 playoff team)
Week 5 @ Ravens (2020 playoff team)
Week 6 Host Texans (AFC South division game)
Week 7 @ 49ers
Week 8 Host Titians (AFC South division game)

The Colts play six games versus 2020 playoffs teams in their first 8 weeks of the season. The Colts clearly have shortchanged their offerings to the scheduling gods. The week 7 game drags the Colts all the way to west cost to play the 49ers. The 49ers roster is dynamic on both sides of the ball. The contest on the field will be just as stressful as flight for the Colts. In week 8 the Colts host the Titians. Last season, Indianapolis placed second to Tennessee in the AFC South division. The Colts may not have much fuel in their tank after week 8. I also worry that Colts will not respect the Jets the way they did most of their previous opponents.

The Colts will be favored in this contest. The line should be Colts -6. Unless the Jets go 0-17 on the season, they win a game somewhere. I suggest betting the Jets on the moneyline for a strait up. Your odds for the Jets win will be almost 2 to 1. Adding more points to their spread in a teaser is the move to make.

WEEK 9

Texans @ Dolphins

In week 9, the Miami Dolphins play host to the Houston Texans. The Dolphins need a schedule boost after playing the Buffalo Bills (2020 AFC runner up) in week 8. It seems that to scheduling guys answered the call on behalf of the Miami Dolphins in week 9. We will first look over to Houston Texans schedule.

Week 6 @ Colts (2020 playoff team) (AFC South division game)
Week 7 @ Cardinals
Week 8 Host Rams (2020 playoff team)

Once the Texans reach week 9, they will be playing their third road game in four weeks. In fact, the Dolphins will be third 2020 playoff team that Texans will face as well. Week 9 could be the moment in which all the elite competition crushes the Texans.

The Dolphins will be favored in this contest. The point spread should be Dolphins -6.5. The spread could bet set as high as Dolphins -8. I love the Dolphins to win the game.

I do believe the Dolphins are perfect to be in a teaser spot. Increase the Dolphins value moving their spread down in a teaser.

WEEK 9

Titians @ Rams (Sunday Night Football)

The Rams host The Titans in the Week 9 Sunday Football Game. Tennessee will be playing back-to-back road games. It's time we put our eyes the Titans schedule.

Week 6 Host Bills (2020 AFC runner up)
Week 7 Host Chiefs (2020 AFC Champions)
Week 8 @ Colts (2020 playoff team)
Week 9 @ Rams (2020 Playoff Team)

The schedule offers the Titans no room to breathe. Tennessee plays four consecutive 2020 playoffs teams The Chiefs and Bills ranked # 1 and #2 respectively in the AFC. The latter two games are on the road. The Titans and Colts game in week 8, is an AFC South showdown for supremacy. The miles traveled from Tennessee to Los Angeles, is yet another hurdle for the Titans to clear.

The Rams will be home favorites. I am anticipating a line Rams -4.5. My advice is back the Rams in this spot. It's human nature for Tennessee to play under their abilities. The Rams should be in your teaser also.

The Titans will be on back-to-back games, and Rams will have a home crowd stoked with passion for the Sunday night game.

WEEK 10

WEEK 10

Buccaneers @ Washington Football Team

The good news for the Washington Football team is they will have a bye in week 9. The bad news is that the Buccaneers also have a bye in week 9. The schedule is oh so unkind to Washington. This is a rematch of the 2020 Wild Card playoff round game. Tampa Bay thumped Washington 31-23 knocking them out the playoffs. I cannot bet against Tampa Bay in mid-season form fresh of a bye. This a crappy hand dealt to Washington.

The Point spread could be Buccaneers -8.5. The Buccaneers points will be inflated as the sportsbook do not want to pay out on Buccaneers tickets every week. I will move the Buccaneers down in a teaser. This spread will be difficult to cover unless Brady and company jump out the gates in Washington.

WEEK 10
Eagles @ Broncos

The Broncos tread a demanding trail of opponents going prior to week 10.

Week 6 Host Raiders (AFC West division game)
Week 7 @ Browns (2020 playoff team)
Week 8 Host Washington (2020 playoff team)
Week 9 @ Cowboys

I do believe these teams will have the Broncos prepared to play at home against the Eagles. These four teams are quality opponents. However, the combination is not overbearing with difficulty to work against the Broncos.

Philadelphia will be playing their third road game in four weeks.

Week 7 @ Raiders
Week 8 @ Lions
Week 9 Host Chargers
Week 10 @ Broncos

I say this is disadvantage for 2nd year QB Jalen Hurts and his unproven offensive unit.

The high altitude in Denver is factor visiting teams most adjust to. With the Eagles playing third road games in four weeks, the altitude will work in the Broncos favor.

This is a very good spot to bet the Broncos as a home favorite. I anticipate -4. or -4.5 Broncos. I advise is betting on the Broncos. This spot is built to insert the Broncos fit well into a teaser also.

WEEK 10
Saints @ Titians

In 2020, The Saints and the Titians earned playoff berths with impressive regular season performances. I normally like to consider betting on Tennessee when playing home games. When hosting the Saints in week 10, The Titians will be playing their fifth consecutive playoff team. Let's view this path for the Titians.

Week 6 Host Bills (2020 AFC runner up)
Week 7 Host Chiefs (2020 AFC champion)
Week 8 @ Colts (AFC South division game) (2020 playoff team)
Week 9 @ Rams (2020 playoff team)

I just do not like this spot for Tennessee. Including their week 10 contest with the Saints. The Titans play five consecutive 2020 playoffs teams. In week 6 the Titans play the Bills. The Bills lost in the AFC Champion to Chiefs.

In Week 7, the Titans play the Chiefs. Kansas City has played in the last Super Bowls. In Week 8, Tennessee plays against the Colts in Indianapolis. Last season Titans and Colts both compiled 11-5 records. In week 9, the Titans have a road game in Los Angles verses the Rams. The Rams are the current favorite to Win the NFC West.

The Saints enter Week 10 playing two consecutive NFC South teams. Win or loss these two consecutive divisional games will strain a team's emotions and focus. However, the Saints get to play these two games at home and then fly to Tennessee for the Titians game.

The Titans will be home Favorites. The Titans will be a popular team that the public will be betting on weekly. The line could be set at Titians -5.5. I advise that you bet the Saints and on the point spread. Adding more points to the Saints in your teaser is a wise move as well. The Saints moneyline hold value as a low risk- high reward wager.

WEEK 10
Vikings @Chargers

The Los Angles Chargers aim to defend their home as the Minnesota Vikings sail into town during week 11. Each squad enters the season with similar talent levels. This matchup is a token example on why I use the schedule to gain deeper insight. Vegasinsider.com projects the Vikings to win 8.5 games. The Chargers season win total sits at 9.

Unfortunately for Minnesota, The Vikings receive the short end of the stick from the schedule makers.

Week 10 @Ravens (2020 playoff team)
Week 11 @ Chargers

The Vikings week 10 contest takes them all the way east to play the Ravens in Baltimore. The Ravens return the #1 ranked team rushing offense. The Ravens grind down opposing defenses. The residual affect will linger with the Vikings into the following week.

Minnesota plays on the East Coast standard time zone in Baltimore.

In week 11, Minnesota must fly to the Los Angles on the west coast to duel with the Chargers. The Viking will now be playing on the Pacific standard time zone. The shift of time zones will alter the rhythm of the Vikings.

Let's look at the Chargers schedule.

Week 7 Bye
Week 8 Host Patriots
Week 9 @ Eagles

Los Angles plays at Philadelphia verses the Eagles in week 10. The Chargers will experience a drawn-out flight to the east coast and back home to L.A. I find the Charges bye in week 7 to soften the blow of milage incurred by playing in Philadelphia. Los Angles plays one road game and returns home. Minnesota most endure back-to-back games grueling road trips.

The Chargers should be -3 favorites. I do not want the points with the Vikings. The is a dubious spot for Minnesota. Bet the Chargers on spread. Los Angeles plays at home. The Vikings on back-to-back Rd games, sustains a fourth quarter advantage.

WEEK 11

WEEK 11

Washington Football @ Panthers

The Carolina Panthers host the Washington Football Team in week 11. Midway through the regular season I look for all details to the schedule point me to winner. Let's have look at the Panthers schedule.

Weeks 7-10 issues the Carolina Panthers three road games in four weeks. However, none of the Panthers opponents during this run played in the 2020 playoffs.

Week 7 @ Giants
Week 8 @ Falcons (NFC South division game)
Week 9 Host Patriots
Week 10 @ Cardinals

I do believe the week 10 road game at Arizona will linger into week 11. The difference in climate and time zone differences cannot be ignored. The Cardinals passing attack will test the fabric of the Panthers defensive unit.

The Panthers are further ahead on offense than defense. In 2021 Ownership is spending about 61 million on their defense, $86 million on their offensive payroll.

After a week 10 game hosting the Buccaneers, Washington will welcome the Panthers group on defense.

I expect Carolina to be the favorite. I foresee a point spread of Panthers -2. You want to place the Washington Football Team in a teaser and move their spread up.

WEEK 11

Patriots @ Falcons (Thursday Night Football)

This Thursday Night Football game will have the Falcons and Patriots playing of three days rest. At this stage of the season New England plans to return to their winning ways. Atlanta's intentions for 2021 remain a mystery.

I am uncomfortable with the fact that they the Patriots will be playing their third road game in four weeks. Let's take a glance at the Patriots schedule.

Week 8 @ Chargers
Week 9 @ Panthers
Week 10 Host Browns

The Patriots will be road favorites maybe as high -4.5. Public money will be flooding in on the Patriots and they will let you know the Falcons play is hotter. The schedule says take the points with the Falcons. I will add the New England will have not had a bye week yet, the Falcons bye was back in week 6. The Falcons money line is a strong play for betters looking for plus money.

WEEK 11
49ers @Jagaurs

In week 11, the Jacksonville Jaguars play host to the San Francisco 49ers. The two clubs' goals for 2020 season are opposites. After a disastrous 2020 season, San Francisco wants contending for a playoff spot. The Jacksonville franchise earned the #1 overall pick in this year's draft, using number 1 overall pick to rebuild.

The 49ers play to a couple games that are an area of concern prior to week 11.

Week 9 Host Cardinals (NFC West division game)
Week 10 Host Rams (2020 playoff team) (NFC West division game)

San Francisco plays two consecutive division games before traveling to Jacksonville. The 49ers will have to have channel high vibrations in both contests. The Rams game is the Monday Night Football game. I fear the 49ers will get powered up for The Rams and then flatline for the Jaguars. The 49ers flight to Jacksonville is extensive and taxing, The 49ers will have to shift their bodies form Pacific to Eastern standard time.

The Jaguars face a gauntlet, playing three consecutive playoff team prior to the 49ers. Hers is the Jaguars schedule.

Week 8 @ Seahawks (2020 playoff team)
Week 9 Host Bills (2020 AFC runner up)
Week 10 @ Colts (2020 playoff team) (AFC South division game)

This is an imposing series of games the young Jaguars. However, after playing three playoff teams, the Jaguars won't be shell shocked by the talent of the 49ers. The 49er will be a heavy road favorite against the Jaguars.

The high voltage the 49ers expend in weeks 9 and 10 combined with the extensive flight to Jacksonville. I still find the Jaguars to be holding the trump cards to cover the point spread.

A winning 49ers squad will have this point spread overinflated.

This line could get as high as 49ers –10. I think it will open closer 49ers –8. I do not find this to be a prime spot for San Francisco. If you bet this game, the schedule says take the points with the Jaguars. This is also a good spot to look the placing a Jacksonville Jaguars money line bet.

WEEK 11
Ravens @ Dolphins

The Ravens take flight to the windy city to take on the Bears. This contest features a pair of clubs that both played themselves into the 2020 Playoffs.

The Ravens face the Dolphins in Miami in week 10. The climate change will disrupt the Ravens physically. The Ravens play in Chicago a week later. Climate conditions in Miami and Chicago are like attempting to compare apples to oranges.

In week 10, the Bears will be resting on their bye week. Chicago will receive a full week to compose a strategy to slow down Lamar Jackson and the Ravens. Bears head coach Matt Nagy is 0-2 against the spread coming of a bye week. Coach Nagy does receive aid with Ravens playing back-to-back road games.

I anticipate the Ravens to be -5 favorites. I won't be shocked if the line gets as high as Ravens - 6. I do see enough in the schedule two tease the Chicago point spread up. The Bears are worth a look on the money line to pull off a straight win. I am applying that the risk is worth the reward with the Bears.

I have the home team fresh off a bye week. The visiting Baltimore team, playing back-to-back games in two completely different sets of climates. If you have a parlay or round Robin of plus money underdogs, the Bears should have a spot in there bet.

WEEK 12

WEEK 12

Raiders @ Cowboys (Thanksgiving Day)

The Raiders visit the Cowboys for a Thanksgiving Day showdown. Both squads will be on a short week playing on just three days of the rest. I am focusing on the previous opponents of Dallas and the Las Vegas to find an advantage.

Dallas plays at the Kansas City Chiefs in Week 11. Arrowhead stadium in Kansas City can take its toll in the visiting Cowboys. The Chiefs will hold the Cowboys accountable by making them play all four quarters.

Las Vegas will be at home playing host to Cincinnati. The Bengals are a far weaker team than Chiefs. The Raider have the luxury of playing at home, with three days of rest before the Thanksgiving Day game.

The Raiders will be the underdog and this spot provides them value. The deal breaker is the fact the this will be the Cowboys third home game in the past weeks. I say the schedule still favors Dallas. If the spread is Dallas -3, I would take the Cowboys on the money line to just win. At -3 a game that should be close is leaving you open for a push.

WEEK 12
Falcons @ Jaguars

The Jaguars host the Falcons during a week 12 showdown in Jacksonville. This game will not draw much interest from them media. However, with this game on the board there is still money to be made.

This home game against the Falcons marks the Jaguars three home game in four weeks.

Week 9 Host Bills (2020 AFC runner up)
Week 10 @ Colts (2020 playoff team)
Week 11 Host 49ers

Jacksonville faces two 2020 Playoff teams and what should a much-improved 49ers group. In this spot the quality of teams played is a positive aspect for Jacksonville. Playing high quality teams will have them sharp to face a team with similar talent.

The Falcons will face a team who could be also looking for its first when in the week window. I do not anticipate the Falcons being set as the favorite. The schedule greatly favors Jacksonville in this spot.

Linemakers should set the Jaguars as the favorite. The spread should be Jaguars -3. My advice to bet on the Jaguars to get the strait up win on the moneyline.

WEEK 12
Panthers @ Dolphins

The Carolina Panthers visit the Miami Dolphins.

This will be the Dolphins third home game in four weeks. In this four-week window, the Dolphins face one AFC East divisional opponent, and one 2020 playoff team.

Week 9 Host Texans
Week 10 Host Ravens (2020 playoff team)
Week 11 @ Jets (AFC East division game)

The Dolphins host their third home game in four weeks as the Panthers take a flight to Miami. The Dolphins schedule is not very demanding, The Ravens are the only opponent in this group that won more than half of their games a year ago. In 2020, The Dolphins went 10-6 overall and 5-3 at home.

I find this be a prime spot for the Dolphins. Miami will be set as the favorite. I project a line of Dolphins -5. I am down to bet the Dolphins point spread no higher than -5.5. In a teaser bet, I suggest teasing the Dolphins down. This is prime spot for Miami.

WEEK 12

Bills @ Saints (Sunday Night Football)

The Week 12 Sunday Night Football features the Buffalo Bills at the New Orleans Saints. Last season the Bills and Saints won their respective divisions. Buffalo is now a team that will haunted in the AFC. The Saints aim to return to the post season without the services of the recently retired Drew Brees.

After playing two straight games on the road, the Saints will be playing back home again in New Orleans. The Saints will play week 10 at the Tennessee Titans (2020 Playoff team) and Week 11 at the Philadelphia Eagles. I find the road milage accrued in these two games to be moderate for The Saints.

The Buffalo Bills will be playing the back end of three road games in four weeks. Here is the schedule of weeks 9-11 for Buffalo

Week 9 @ Jaguars
Week 10 @ Jets (AFC East division game)
Week 11 Host Colts (2020 playoff team)
Week 12 @ Saints (2020 playoff team)

I will not ignore the fact the Bills are playing away from for the third time in four weeks. The Bills could be on roll and win all three games prior to playing the Saints.

Buffalo may be in line for a letdown.

Most gamblers bet on the Sunday Night Football game simply because it is the only game on. Do not be so fast to assume a public favorite like the Bills are a lock Bet.

The Bills may be a road favorite. However, a Saints team with a winning record would be the favorite. Either way I cannot see either side being favored by more than 3 points.

The schedule is nudging me to bet The Saints. I say take the points with New Orleans as a home underdog. If the Saints are -3 to -3.5 home favorites. then bet the Saints. I do not at all advise betting the Bills to cover any points in this spot.

WEEK 12

Vikings @ 49ers

The Minnesota Vikings hosts the San Francisco 49ers in Week 12. Vegasinsider. com list the 49ers win total at 10.5, the Vikings win total is set at 8.5. This game consists of two offensive groups that can really move the ball and score points.

This spot does not look so hot for the Vikings. Minnesota will be playing their third road game in four weeks. We will have look at the Vikings schedule.

Week 9 @ Ravens (2020 playoff team)
Week 10 @ Chargers
Week 11 Host Packers (2020 playoff team) (NFC North playoff game)
Week 12 @49ers

Here we have quality of opponents and logistic working against the Vikings. In week 9 Minnesota must go east to play the Ravens. Baltimore will does not yield home losses without great force.

In week 10, the Vikings fly west to play the Chargers in Los Angeles. The Packers invade Minnesota in week 11.

Green Bay and Minnesota are historic bitter rivals and both teams will leave their hearts on the field. In week 12, the Vikings fly back out West to San Francisco to play the 49ers. The schedule offers the Vikings no breaks weeks 9–12.

The 49ers will be playing their third home game in four weeks.

Week 9 Host Cardinals (NFC West division game)
Week 10 Host Rams (2020 playoff team) NFC West division game)
Week 11 @ Jaguars
Week 12 Host Vikings

In weeks 9 and 10, the 49ers play back-to-back NFC West division games. The fact that these are both home games for San Francisco ease the collective stress. In week 11, the 49ers make a terribly long flight to Jacksonville to play the Jaguars. The 49ers have deal with less scheduling resistance than the Vikings.

Linemakers wet set San Francisco as the favorite. I see line being set at 49ers -5.5. I love this spot for San Francisco. For those of you that like to place first half wagers. The 49ers first half bet is in play here. The 49ers should surely be in your teaser.

WEEK 13

WEEK 13

WEEK 13
Eagles @ Jets

In week 13, The Eagles visits the Jets. Neither team enjoyed a successful 2020 season. New York posted a 2-14 record. Philadelphia complied a 5-11 mark. I am interested to see if either team has created a winning culture.

The New York Jets will play their third home game in four weeks.

Week 10 Host Bills (2020 AFC runner up) (AFC East division game)
Week 11 Host Dolphins (2020 playoff team) (AFC East division game)
Week 12 @ Texans
Week 13 Host Eagles

New York plays two consecutive AFC division games. Week 10 versus the Bills and week 11 against the Dolphins. The Bills and Dolphins are 2020 playoff qualifiers. At least the Jets will get to play these two games at home.

Philadelphia will be on the road for third time in four weeks.

Week 10 @ Broncos
Week 11 Host Saints (2020 playoff team)
Week 12 @ Giants
Week 13 @ Jets

The Eagles are young offense with no proven veteran leadership. Their defense is not commodity either. Weeks 10-13 will determine if the Eagles will end the season playing for wins or draft picks. I surely do not trust them in this week 13 spot.

The Jets should be installed as the favorite. I believe point spread should be Jets -2.5. This is spot bet on the Jets with the point spread. A first half wager on the Jets is another sound move. I advise placing the Jets in a teaser bet.

WEEK 13
Chargers @ Bengals

In week 13, The Bengals host the Chargers. Two of the NFL's rising star quarterbacks will be on display. Cincinnati drafted QB Joe Burrows with the #1 overall pick in the 2020 draft. Five spots later, The Los Angeles Chagres selected QB Justin Herbert with the #6 overall pick.

We start with a brief rundown of the Chargers week 12 scenario.

Los Angeles will play a heated game on the road versus the Denver Broncos, an AFC West rival. The Chargers will also have to recover from the thin air and high altitude in Denver and make the extended flight for Los Angles to Cincinnati.

In week 13, the Bengals will play their fourth road game in five weeks. This stretch of home cooking includes a bye in week 10.

Week 9 Host Browns (2020 playoff Team) (AFC North division game)
Week 10 Bye Week
Week 11 @Raiders
Week 12 Host Steelers (2020 playoff Team) (AFC North division game)
Week 13 Host Chargers

The Bengals could lose all three of their games in weeks 9-12. Under these circumstances the Bengals would be in line for a victory in 13 versus the Chargers.

Linemakers should set the Chargers as the favorite. The point spread could get set at Chargers -3.5. I advise betting the Bengals to outright win on the money line. This is risk versus reward play to collect plus money with Cincinnati. Capitalize on the Bengals benefitting from playing their fourth home game in five weeks.

WEEK 14

WEEK 14

WEEK 14
Saints @ Jets

William Hill Sports Book sets the Jets win total at over/under 6 games. This Week 14 game verse the Saints may be one of the Jets wins. New Orleans will have to prove they can win on the road and cover the spread as a favorite.

In week 14, the New York Jets will be playing their third home game in four Weeks.

The Saints schedule week 10 -13 provides troublesome circumstances.

Week 10 @ Titians (2020 playoff team)
Week 11 @ Eagles
Week 12 Host Bills (2020 AFC runner up) (2020 playoff team)
Week 13 Host Cowboys

Although New Orleans could be underdogs versus the Bills and Cowboys, The Bills flex a potent offense and a stout defense. The Cowboys offensive unit is electric takes no take prisoners. Once Dallas gets a hold of your secondary, they will continue to score touchdowns and build a lead. I can see the Saints being grinned down physically and lacking the spark they need to play the Jets.

The Saints should be installed as the favorite. I am anticipating a point spread of Saints -5. Placing the Jets in a teaser bet also aligns well with this spot for the Jets.

WEEK 14

49ers @ Bengals

The Bengals host the 49ers in Week 14. Cincinnati has the pieces to field a dynamic offense. San Francisco will be looking to grab a win and get back home. This spot marks the third road game in four weeks for the 49ers.

Week 11 @ Jaguars
Week 12 Host Vikings
Week 13 @ Seahawks (2020 playoff team) (NFC South division game)
Week 14 @ Bengals

Week 14, the 49ers to travel out east from San Francisco for the second time in four weeks. San Francisco's week 13 clash with The Seahawks may burn to much steam out of the 49ers. Seattle boasts one of the most rambunctious crowds in the league

The 49ers /Seahawks is also the Sunday Night Football game of week 13. I am afraid the 49ers will leave to much of themselves in Seattle.

The Bengals on the other hand will be playing their third straight game at home. Consecutive home games become quite a luxury this late in the season. This is very strong spot for the Bengals.

The 49ers will set as road favorites. The points given to Cincinnati with the spread are at a premium The 49ers could be favored as high as -8.5. Add more points with the Bengals in a teaser. This is a prime plus money opportunity with the Bengals. The Bengals are worth a shot for as straight-up win on the moneyline.

WEEK 14

Lions @ Broncos

The Lions host the Broncos during week 14. Thi contest will fly under the radar. With the proper attention you can mine gold in these types of games. Let's first evaluate the Lions schedule.

Week 11 @ Browns (2020 playoff team)
Week 12 Host Bears (2020 playoff team) (NFC North division game)
Week 13 Host Vikings (NFC North division game)

We see the Lions must withstand a brutal series of games of here. The Browns will be load for the Lions at home In Cleveland. How will the Lions respond to their back-to-back NFC South Division games? The Lions do not a winning culture, and this team might not be on point when they reach Denver. Detroit will also have to adjust to the thin air and high altitude in Denver.

Now let check out the Broncos schedule

Week 10 Host Eagles
Week 11 Bye week
Week 12 Host Chargers (AFC West division game)
Week 13 @Cheifs (2020 playoff team) (AFC West division game)

Denver plays back-to-back division games in weeks 12 and 13. The Broncos host the Chargers in week 12. In week 13, Denver makes a vaunted road trip to Kansas City to battle the Chiefs. Home field advantage is imperative for the Broncos in this contest with the Lions. The Broncos spend four of five weeks in Denver, including a bye in week 11.

The Broncos will be the favorite, I figure the line will set at Broncos -5, betting the Broncos is the play here. I do believe that the Broncos at -5 are sound move to put in your teaser, moving the Broncos spread down. The Lions schedule gives Detroit little to no help.

WEEK 15

WEEK 15
Packers @ Ravens

The Ravens host the 2020 NFC North Champion Packers in a late season week 15 contest. The Ravens will be grinding towards a third consecutive playoff appearance.

First let's have glance at the Packers schedule.

Week 12 Host Rams (2020 playoff team)
Week 13 Bye Week
Week 14 Host Bears (2020 playoff team) (NFC North division game)

The Rams are stifling test for the Packers in week 12. Los Angeles employs multiple formations on offense, this causes defense to spend extra time in the film room.

In week 13, Green Bay will then have much welcome bye. Week 14, consist of an intense home game versus the Chicago Bears. The Bears and Packers NFC North rivalry stands has thread to the fabric of the NFL. Win, lose or draw; the Packers will need to reset themselves before reaching Baltimore.

I should be loving the Ravens in this spot. Yet when I read Baltimore's schedule, I am forced to reevaluate my position.

Week 12 Host Browns (2020 playoff team) (AFC North division game)
Week 13 @ Steelers (2020 playoff team) (AFC North division game)
Week 14 @ Browns (2020 playoff team) (AFC North division game)

The Ravens, Browns and Steelers all participated in the 2020 NFL playoffs. The Ravens will expend immense levels of emotions in all three of these ball games. In Fact, this run will make or break the Ravens season. How much emotional fuel will the Ravens have left in reserve?

The Ravens will be the favorite in this game. You should add more points with Packers in a teaser. The Ravens will be playing on fumes in this game. If Baltimore builds a 10 or more-point lead, they will not be able to sustain in the second half. The line should be Ravens -4. My suggestion is to bet the Ravens to win on the money line.

WEEK 15
Patriots @Colts

In week 15, the Patriots visit the Colts in Indianapolis. The Colts finished the 2020 season with a 11-5 record earning a trip to the playoffs. Last year's Patriots produced an unfamiliar 7-9 record.

We will examine New England schedule first.

Week 11@ Falcons
Week 12 Host Titians (2020 Playoff Team)
Week 13 @ Bills (2020 AFC runner Up) (AFC East division game)
Week 14 Bye

Week 12 at the Tennessee Titians will be a rugged affair for the Patriots. The Titians return the NFL's #2 ranked game The Bills and Patriots both play in AFC East Division. The Bills won the division in 2020 and fell one game short of a Super Bowl appearance. New England does however receive a bye in week 14.

The Colts must also play a distressing schedule prior to week 15.

Week 11 @ Bills (2020 AFC runner up)
Week 12 Host Buccaneers (2020 Super Bowl champions)
Week 13 @ Texans (AFC South division game)
Week 14 Bye

The Colt's play in Buffalo versus the Bills (2020 AFC runner up). The following week, the Colts host the defending Super Champion Tampa Bay Buccaneers. In week 13, Indy travels south for an AFC South Division game with the Houston Texans. A bye week during Week 14, serves as the light at the end of the tunnel for the Colts.

Both the Patriots and Colts experience byes in week 14. New England head coach Bill Belichick is 13-9 against the spread off a bye week. Colts head coach Frank Reich is 2-0 against the spread of a bye week.

The point spread in this game should be close. Perhaps the line will be set at Colts -2.5. I do not see enough help on the schedule to favor either squad in terms of the point spread. I do believe that The Colts hold power placing their spread in a teaser bet.

WEEK 16

WEEK 16

49ers @ Titians (Thursday Night Football)

The Tennessee Titans host the San Francisco 49ers in week 16. The Titians ended the 2020 regular season on tear, earning a playoff berth. San Francisco's quest to reach the post season was derailed by injuries. The 49ers look to reclaim 2019 Super Bowl runner up form.

This will be the tail end of three road game in four weeks for 49ers. Late in the season these are undesired circumstance for 49ers. Now let's put our eyes on the 49ers schedule.

Week 13 @ Seahawks (2020 playoff Team) (NFC South division game)
Week 14 @ Bengals
Week 15 Host Falcons
Week 16@Titains (2020 playoff team)

While the 49ers weeks 13-16 are loaded with road games, the Titans schedule is home friendly. This stretch of home cooking for Tennessee also includes bye in week 13. Here is look at the Titians schedule.

Week 13 Bye Week
Week 14 Host Jaguars (AFC South division Game)
Week 15 @ Steelers (2020 playoff team)
Week 16 Host 49ers

In week 16, The schedule is far kinder to Titans than it is to the 49ers. On paper both squads are evenly matched. The Titians should a home favorite with a – 3 point spread. I suggest betting the Titians. The home /road contrast factor should not be ignored. I prefer to apply any teaser points to the home team with Tennessee.

WEEK 16
Jaguars @ Jets

The Jacksonville Jaguars hosts the New York Jets. This contest features the NFL's next generation star Quarterbacks. Jacksonville selected QB Trevor Lawrence with the #1 overall pick in this year's draft. With the very next pick in the 2021 draft, The Jets used the #2 overall pick on QB Zack Wilson.

The Jets will be playing their third home game in four weeks.

Week 13 Host Eagles
Week 14 Host Saints (2020 playoff team)
Week 15@ Dolphins (2020 playoff Team) (AFC East division game)

The Jets encounter resistance in weeks 14 and 15. The Saints and Dolphins each finished 2020 with top 10 scoring defenses. The Jets will appreciate playing a Jacksonville a team with equal talent. New York is gifted this game to played at home with the Jaguars.

Jacksonville will be playing their third road game in four weeks. This is what the Jaguars schedule look like.

Week 13 @ Rams (2020 playoff team)
Week 14 @ Titians (2020 playoff team) (AFC South division game)
Week 15 Host Texans (AFC South division game)

The week 13 road game at the Los Angeles Rams offers is no easy task. The Jags will shift to multiple time zones, from Eastern Standard to Pacific Standard time zone. The Rams boast one of the most balanced rosters in football and will be heavy favorites in the contest.

The Titians game is an AFC South division game. Tennessee will show no mercy on the young Jaguars. The Titans are the defending AFC South champs. Next, Jacksonville hosts the Texans in a second consecutive divisional contents.

The Jets should be set as the favorite. I can see the line opening at Jets -2. You bet the Jets in this scenario on the point spread. I find placing the Jaguars in a teaser as to have stellar value. Maximize the Jets spot of playing their third home game in four weeks.

WEEK 17

WEEK 17

WEEK 17
Dolphins @ Titians

The Tennessee Titans host the Miami Dolphins in a week 17 contests. The Titans and Dolphins each played in the 2020 playoffs. If both teams continue their success from a year ago, then this game will loom large for either team looking to earn a post season berth.

This will be back-to-back row games for the Miami Dolphins. The Titans on the other hand, will be playing at home for the second consecutive week. This will be very strong spot for the Titans. With just two games remaining in the regular season, I prefer to have the scheduling circumstances of the Titans.

Tennessee will to be set as the favorite. I am anticipating a point spread of Titans −4.5. I advise betting Tennessee on the point spread. You maximize this spot by placing the Titians in a teaser bet.

WEEK 17
Raiders @ Colts

With just two weeks remaining int the regular season, The Raiders leave Las Vegas to play the Indianapolis Colts. This contest may carry playoff implications for both teams. The Colts will be wrapping home a stint of that includes a bye week.

Week 14 Bye Week
Week 15 Host Patriots
Week 16 @ Cardinals
Week 17 Host Raiders

This spot shapes up very well the Colts. Indianapolis does not play a 2020 playoff or divisional opponent during string of games. The Raiders game will have the Colts staying at home three out of four weeks.

The Raiders will suffer significant resistance due the quirks of their schedule

Week 14 @ Chiefs (2020 playoff team) (AFC West division game)
Week 15 @ Browns (2020 playoff team)
Week 16 Host Broncos (AFC West division game)
Week 17 @ Colts (2020 playoff team)

The Raiders will be playing their third road game in four weeks. In week 14, the Raiders visit the Chiefs for an AFC West divisional showdown. In week 15 the Raiders make a lengthy trip out Cleveland to face the Browns. In week 16 the Raiders play the Denver Broncos in an AFC West division game. The Broncos and Raiders may possess the most bitter rivalry in football. The Raiders will be faced with to challenge of leading all their emotion on his field at home against Denver, and they're flying east to play the Colts.

Finally, The Colts will be the third 2020 playoff team that the Raiders play within this four-week window.

The Colts will the set as the favorite at home. I for see a line of Colts -4. I prefer to bet the first half with the Colts in this scenario. Indianapolis should be able to get out the gates faster than Las Vegas. Placing the Colt in a teaser bet is the sharpest bet you can make.

WEEK 17
Rams @ Ravens

The Los Angles visit the Baltimore Ravens in week 17. The Ravens and the Rams both view themselves as 2021 Super Bowl contenders. With both teams healthy this game will hold the keys a drive a success post season push.

Let have a look Rams schedule.

Week 14 @ Cardinals (NFC West division game)
Week 15 Host Seahawks (2020 playoff team) (NFC West division game)
Week 16 @ Vikings
Week 17 @ Ravens (2020 playoff team)

Los Angles will play NFC West division games in weeks 14 and 15. Divisional games are always an area of concern. The Cardinals QB Kyler Murray and Seahawks QB Russell Wilson are two of most prolific playmakers in the league. Next, Los Angeles travels to the Midwest to play the Vikings in week 16. Finally in week 17, the miles logged to the Rams extended to the east coast to play in Baltimore.

With both teams healthy the Ravens will be home favorite. The line should be set at Ravens -3. I advise betting the Ravens on the money line. In a teaser bet you can fortify the strength of this spot for Baltimore moving their spread down.

Printed in the United States
by Baker & Taylor Publisher Services